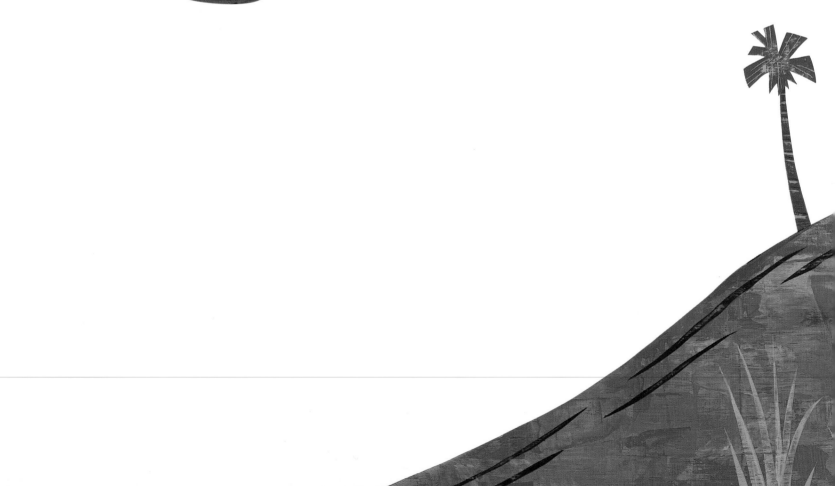

PAM MUÑOZ RYAN

Our California

ILLUSTRATED BY
RAFAEL LÓPEZ

Charlesbridge

Welcome to

California!

There are valleys, deserts, mountains, and coast.
Which region do you think that you will like most?

Yosemite

Coloma

Sacramento

San Francisco

Sonoma

Eureka

DEATH VALLEY

GREAT CENTRAL VALLEY

Palm Springs

San Juan Capistrano

San Diego

Los Angeles

Monterey

CHANNEL ISLANDS

Start in the south of this golden land,
in fair **San Diego,** where vistas are grand.
In this coastal city, there's plenty to do.
Surf, swim, and sun, then visit the zoo.

San Juan Capistrano is where you will learn
about a quaint village where swallows return.
Junípero Serra stopped here on his way
to build a grand mission from adobe clay.

Next is **Los Angeles** and famed Hollywood.
You can visit the places where movie stars stood.
This "City of Angels" has lots to explore:
tar pits, museums, and amusements galore.

Now, the **Channel Islands!** Take a boat out
and cruise these blue waters to glimpse a whale's spout.
Here in the Pacific, among the kelp strips,
are playful sea otters and the ghosts of old ships.

As you travel north and approach **Monterey,**
see the bold, craggy rocks that surround the bay.
When sardines were plenty, some years ago,
the day's catch was sold on Cannery Row.

Stop in "The City." **San Francisco's** the name.
Here morning fog lingers and winds bring the rain.
Cable cars hurry up one hill and down,
and tourists eat lunch in old Chinatown.

Once in **Sonoma,** under rebel command,
settlers claimed a republic for Destiny's Land.
They made a new flag to be flown everywhere
with one stripe, one star, and a fierce grizzly bear.

This state has a motto from prospectors' lore.
They yelled it when spotting that rich golden ore.
"Eureka!" they cheered. What a jubilant sound!
It's also the name of this northwestern town.

Hello, **Sacramento,** and the capitol dome.
This delta city is the governor's home.
The Pony Express once delivered the mail
from a post in Missouri to the end of the trail.

Here in **Coloma,** as the story is told,
James W. Marshall discovered pure gold.
The forty-niners came and mined every hill
and panned every stream that was near Sutter's Mill.

Now east to **Yosemite**, where sequoias abound and magnificent monoliths rise from the ground. Once, ice-age glaciers carved their way through and created a valley with a breathtaking view.

The **Great Central Valley,** with its plentiful yields,
feeds the whole nation from its orchards and fields.
This rich, thirsty farmland needs water to thrive.
Canals, pumps, and dams keep this valley alive.

PRODUCE

In **Death Valley's** desert of salt pan and sand,
dust devils twirl across wild, crusty land.
Here's Furnace Creek, a sweltering spot.
It's over one-twenty! Are you getting hot?

Finally **Palm Springs** and the end of the ride.
Put up your feet and enjoy the poolside.
Sit back and relax from the travel routine
and remember the treasure-filled places you've seen.

Many historians think the name California comes from a romantic Spanish fiction story called "Las Sergas de Esplandián" ("The Exploits of Esplandián") by Garcí Ordóñez de Montalvo, published in 1510. The story is about an imaginary, treasure-filled island called California that was not far from "Terrestrial Paradise" and was ruled by Queen Calafia. When Spanish explorers discovered the Pacific Coast north of Mexico, sometime in the 1530s or 1540s, they called it California after the island in the story.

State flag

State insect
Dogface butterfly

State seal

State animal
Grizzly bear

State flower
Golden poppy

State mineral
Gold

State bird
Quail

State tree
Great redwood

State marine mammal
Gray whale

San Diego

* Thousands of years ago Asian hunters migrated to North America through what is now Alaska. Their descendants, the first Californians, later became known as Native Americans.
* In the 1500s, Juan Rodríguez Cabrillo landed in San Diego and claimed the area for Spain. Later San Diego became the site of the first West Coast settlement, on Presidio Hill. Today this area has been restored in Old Town State Park.
* Eucalyptus trees from Australia were planted in San Diego in the 1860s for their hard wood and oil. They are now a distinctive feature of San Diego's landscape.
* Many ships have stopped in San Diego's harbor over the past 400 years. Today it is home to a U.S. Navy port.
* The vintage wooden Giant Dipper Roller Coaster in Mission Beach is a National Historic Landmark.
* Poinsettia plants are grown at the Paul Ecke Poinsettia Ranch in Encinitas, north of San Diego. From there they are shipped to all parts of the nation.

San Juan Capistrano

* Spain sent missionaries to California in 1769 to establish churches and to colonize the Native Americans who lived on the frontier. Junípero Serra, a Spanish priest, is called "the Father of California." He founded nine of the twenty-one missions that reach from San Diego to Sonoma, including San Juan Capistrano. Each mission was built "one day's journey by foot" from the next, along El Camino Real, or "The Royal Road." This road is still marked by the missions' staff-and-bell symbol.
* The Shoshone Indians who lived here were renamed "Juaneño" by the missionaries. Their mission products included cured hides, dipped candles, and soap.
* The swallows of Capistrano leave each year around October 23rd and return the next spring, around the 19th of March.
* San Juan Capistrano, in Orange County, was once surrounded by citrus groves. Today most of the area is housing developments.

Los Angeles

* After landing in San Diego, Cabrillo continued on his voyage and sighted San Pedro, the present harbor of Los Angeles. He saw smoke from the campfires of many Native American villages and called the harbor Bahía de los Fumos (Bay of Smokes).
* In 1781, forty-four Mexican settlers established Pueblo de Nuestra Señora la Reina de Los Angeles de Porciúncula, which means "Town of Our Lady the Queen of the Angels of Porciúncula." Now it is simply called Los Angeles.
* The La Brea pits are bogs of oil and tar that trapped prehistoric animals in this area. Thousands of fossils have been recovered from the tar pits, including the saber-toothed tiger, the state fossil.
* Since 1890, the Tournament of Roses Parade has been an annual New Year's Day event in Pasadena. It includes elaborate floats decorated with flowers.
* Griffith Park, home of Griffith Observatory, is the largest urban park in California.
* The endangered California condor lives along the central coastal mountains, from Monterey County to north Los Angeles County.

Channel Islands

* The Channel Islands stretch off the coast of California from Santa Barbara to the San Clemente area. Writer Scott O'Dell wrote about the island of San Nicolas in his famous novel, *Island of the Blue Dolphins.*
* Pirates used to visit the Channel Islands. Several shipwrecks lie at the bottom of the sea—some people think there is still sunken treasure there. Many scuba divers still search for it near these islands.
* The waters around these islands were once full of sea otters. Fur trappers hunted them until they were almost extinct. Today biologists have brought otters back to the islands. They hope sea otters will make their home here again.
* The Chumash Indians of this area were known for their canoe-building skills. Their tomols were made with wooden planks that were tied together and caulked with tar. These canoes, which were painted red, were strong enough to withstand the Pacific Ocean waters.

Monterey

* One of the first Spanish settlers in Monterey was Gaspar de Pórtola, who is considered the city's founder.
* Around 1777, Monterey became the capital of California. It remained the capital under Spanish and Mexican rule.
* When sardines were abundant, fishermen brought their day's catch to canneries on the Monterey wharf. Today this area is the site of the Monterey Aquarium.
* Abalone, a rock-clinging mollusk, is found along the California coast and is valued for its meat and its shell. The shells are lined with an iridescent material called mother-of-pearl.
* During their annual migration thousands of monarch butterflies stop in the pines in Pacific Grove. The trees appear to be "blooming" with butterflies!
* Monterey Jack was the first cheese native to California. It is named for David Jacks, who first produced it near Monterey.
* The artichoke was introduced to California by Italians. The Salinas Valley is the major United States producer of this vegetable. Brussels sprouts are also grown in this Mediterranean-like climate.

San Francisco

* Until it was renamed in 1847, San Francisco was called Yerba Buena, which means "good herb," after the wild mint that grew there.
* The San Francisco cable cars are State Historical Landmarks. They are the only ones left in the world!
* "Mark Twain," which means "two fathoms deep," was a term that Samuel Clemens used while working on Mississippi riverboats. Clemens, who used Mark Twain as his pen name, wrote many stories about California and the West.
* In 1906, an earthquake and fire destroyed much of San Francisco, but its citizens eventually rebuilt the city.
* The phoenix, a mythical bird reborn from its own ashes, is San Francisco's symbol.
* Domingo Ghirardelli began making chocolate in San Francisco in 1852, and you can still watch it being made in Ghirardelli Square.
* San Francisco's Golden Gate Bridge is almost two miles long. Maintenance crews continually refurbish the bridge using 10,000 gallons of orange paint every year.

Sonoma

* The land we call California has been claimed by many people: the Native Americans, the Spanish, the Mexicans, and the American settlers.
* "Manifest destiny" was a journalistic phrase first used in the 1840s. It meant that the United States should claim the land from the Atlantic Ocean to the Pacific Ocean. This idea fueled arguments between the United States and Mexico about who owned California.
* In 1846, American settlers peacefully took over the Mexican fort in Sonoma from General Mariano Vallejo. They carried a homemade flag featuring a grizzly bear as a symbol of strength and proclaimed California a new republic. This was called the Bear Flag Revolt.
* Since the mid-1800s, Sonoma Valley and Napa Valley have been leaders in California wine making, or viticulture.
* The golden eagle and the bald eagle are native to California. Once there were so many eagles in California that over twenty places were named after them.
* The Coast Miwok, the original inhabitants of the Sonoma area, made thatched willow-framed houses.

Eureka

* Eureka means "I have found it!" in Greek.
* Eureka was founded in 1850 as a gold-mining town. It later became a logging and fishing center.
* In Humboldt Bay you can catch rockfish, Dungeness crab, salmon, shrimp, and oysters.
* In the 1800s, William Carson, a lumber baron, built a large home with a distinctive architecture. Today many houses in the Eureka area are built or preserved in the same Victorian style as the William Carson mansion.
* Redwood National Park is home to the California redwoods. Some are over 1,000 years old and can weigh 500 tons. Although these are the tallest trees in the world, one of their pinecones, which may contain up to sixty seeds, would fit in a tablespoon.
* Many Native American tribes revered the grizzly bear. One tribe of this area, the Hupa, believed that the spirits of grandmothers lived inside the grizzlies. For this reason they never killed them. Due to hunting and trapping by other groups, the grizzly bear is now considered extinct in California.

Sacramento

* Sacramento is the capital of California. The capitol building is surrounded by 800 trees and shrubs from around the world.
* Camellia plants, with their delicate blooms, also flourish in Sacramento, which claims to be the camellia capital of the world.
* Sacramento is located where the American and Sacramento Rivers come together. The Sacramento delta is a triangular plain that has been created from deposits of earth and sand from the rivers. This delta is full of waterways, swamps, marshes, and wet peat: a perfect place to grow produce!
* In the early 1860s, before telephones, telegraphs, or railroads, people in California communicated with those in the rest of the country by Pony Express. Horseback riders relayed messages from the East to Sacramento, the western end of the line.
* In the late 1800s, Theodore Judah hoped to connect the country by transcontinental railroad. He promoted the Central Pacific Railroad Company, which began laying track in Sacramento toward the East.

Coloma

* James W. Marshall and John Sutter went into business together in 1847 to build a sawmill. John Sutter provided land and money, and James Marshall agreed to build the mill. In 1848, before the sawmill was finished, James Marshall discovered gold at the mill site. By 1849, thousands of prospectors had rushed to California to strike it rich. Mining towns cropped up all over the lower mountain elevations, including Oroville, Rough and Ready, Gold Run, El Dorado, and Fiddletown.
* Many people made money by selling goods during the gold rush. At a factory in San Francisco, Levi Strauss made heavy-duty pants out of denim. He reinforced the seams with copper rivets and sold them to miners and farmers. Today they are still known as Levi's® jeans.
* The banjo and the harmonica were familiar musical instruments during the gold rush days. They were easy to cart along, and they brought music and merriment to the sometimes lonesome and difficult lives of the prospectors.

Yosemite

* Yosemite Valley, located in the Sierra Nevada mountains, is known for its rock cliffs and waterfalls. There are more waterfalls in Yosemite than anywhere else in the world!
* A monolith is a single block of stone that is unusually large. Yosemite has monoliths that are the size of mountains. Some of Yosemite's majestic rock forms include Half Dome, Three Brothers, El Capitan, and Cathedral Rocks.
* John Muir, a naturalist who loved the beauty of the outdoors, was dedicated to protecting Yosemite's natural resources.
* Have you ever heard of Hetch Hetchy Valley? It was another beautiful valley in Yosemite, but it could not be protected from development. A dam was built, and the valley is now under water. It has become a reservoir to supply water to San Francisco.
* Yosemite is home to the American black bear, the Steller's jay, and abundant mule deer.
* The Mono Lake Paiutes, a tribe in the Yosemite area, are known for their beautiful, intricate baskets.

Great Central Valley

* The "Great Central Valley," named Valle Grande by the Spanish, is California's prime region for agriculture and livestock. Although it has been called the most fertile farmland in the world, there is little natural water here. The California aqueduct, a series of reservoirs, pumps, and cement channels, carries water over 400 miles from the Sacramento delta to this and other parched areas.
* After working as a laborer in the Central Valley, Cesar Chavez started the National Farm Workers Union. He organized and demonstrated to improve the working conditions of farmworkers.
* Once, approximately fifty tribes of Yokut Indians occupied the Central Valley. One staple of their diet, the acorn, was gathered from oak trees, stored, husked, and then used to make flour for a kind of pudding.
* Oil is one of California's most important industries and resources, especially in the San Joaquin Valley. If you look across the valley, you will see many oil derricks and oil pumps.

Death Valley

* Death Valley is the hottest and driest place in North America. It gets only about 1½ inches of rain per year.
* Here you can stand in Badwater, the lowest point in the Western Hemisphere at 282 feet below sea level. In the distance you can see Mount Whitney, the highest point in the continental United States at 14,494 feet above sea level.
* Borax, a mineral that is mined in Death Valley, is a salt used to make many products, including laundry detergent. Years ago borax was mined and then hauled by twenty-mule teams to the Mojave railroad station.
* Prickly pear cactuses are common in California. They come in many varieties, including Beavertail, Bunny Ears, and Teddy Bear. Some have edible "pears."
* Joshua trees are giant yucca plants that can grow up to fifty feet tall. They have thick, twisted branches with few leaves and giant, waxlike flowers. Joshua Tree National Monument, east of Palm Springs, is a protected area that features these unusual trees.

Palm Springs

* Palm Springs, located in California's Colorado Desert, is a favorite resort town for golfers and people who like warm winters.
* Have you ever felt an earthquake? Earthquakes sometimes occur along the San Andreas Fault. This fault zone runs from Mexico, through California near Palm Springs, and north past Punta Gorda in northern California. Some earthquakes are strong, but most are small and barely noticeable.
* Like streamlined windmills, more than 4,000 wind turbines generate electricity near Palm Springs.
* The town of Indio hosts the annual National Date Festival, which features the exotic fruit of the date palm tree. This event also features camel and ostrich races.
* The Cahuilla Indians lived in this treeless desert area and adapted to the scarce environment. Instead of living on acorns and fish, which weren't plentiful, the Cahuilla lived on seeds, plants, and game. Cahuilla women made tea from mesquite pods and sometimes stored it in an *olla*, or large clay pot.

To my wonderful father, Don Bell. Thank you to Michele Horner and Pat Ward for their assistance with the research for this book.—P. M. R.

For my son Santiago, whose doodles are like maps that whisper of new adventures—R. L.

Published by Charlesbridge
85 Main Street, Watertown, MA 02472
(617) 926-0329
www.charlesbridge.com

Library of Congress Cataloging-in-Publication Data
Ryan, Pam Muñoz.
    Our California / Pam Muñoz Ryan; illustrated by Rafael López.
      p. cm.
    ISBN 978-1-58089-116-5 (reinforced for library use)
    ISBN 978-1-58089-117-2 (softcover)
1. California—Juvenile literature. 2. California—History, Local—Juvenile literature.
3. Cities and towns—California—Juvenile literature. 4. English language—Rhyme—Juvenile literature.
I. López, Rafael, 1961– II. Title.
F861.3.R94 2008
979.4—dc22   2007001474

Printed in Singapore
(hc) 10 9 8 7 6 5 4 3 2
(sc) 10 9 8 7 6 5 4 3

Illustrations painted in acrylics from Mexico and Liquitex Acrylics on grained wood.
    Additional textures made by scraping and distressing the paint.
Display type set in Couchlover, designed by Chank Diesel
Text type set in Weiss
Color transparencies by Gamma One, New York
Color separations by Chroma Graphics, Singapore
Printed and bound November 2010 by Imago in Singapore
Production supervision by Brian G. Walker
Designed by Susan Mallory Sherman